Make Them Choose You

How Local Business Owners Can Double Their Business, Get Customers Consistently, and Have More Free Time WITHOUT Being Held Hostage by Expensive Marketers

Donna Gunter

ORANGE, TX

Make Them Choose You: How Local Business Owners Can Double Their Business, Get Customers Consistently, And Have More Free Time WITHOUT Being Held Hostage by Expensive Marketers -- Donna Gunter. -- 1st ed.
ISBN 978-1-0987593-1-5

This book is dedicated to my mom, Jimmie Helen Wilson Gunter, and my grandparents, Joel Molton Wilson and Nannie Gertrude Holton Wilson, who forever instilled in me (and passed along in my genes) the love of books and reading. I can't imagine living any other way.

BONUSES FOR READERS

As a gift for my readers, I have several book bonuses you can download at:

https://MakeThemChooseYou.com/bonus

Rave Reviews

"I published my book through Kindle Direct Publishing. In order to get it to rise above the crowd, I decided to hire Donna to help me to launch my e-book to see if we could drive it to a best-selling status on the day of the launch. As a result, my book made it to the international best-seller list in two different categories. It not only increased my visibility on Amazon but gave me another reason to share it on my social media. Donna was easy to work with, flexible, and knowledgeable.
- Colleen Russell, The Artful Sage and author of *The Feminine Path to Wholeness: Becoming a Conscious Queen*

"It's not always easy to find passion and professionalism in business but Donna has shown to be both every step of the way. From publishing my first book to strategizing my product launches, Donna has provided the catalyst to my extraordinary new business growth and freely shares what she knows."
- Baruch Spiegel, Educational Consultant and author of *Hope & Change: Building a Better Future for Our Children*

"I would highly recommend Donna Gunter of BizSmart for any of your media and marketing needs. She is amazing. going above and beyond to make her clients a success. Donna is prompt and delivers on all of her promises; as well as making herself available to communicate with whether by phone or email. She never disappoints!"
- Janice Willette, Speaker and author of *Affairs of the Heart: God's Messages to the World*

 *"Donna provides a thorough, knowledgeable and professional service. She takes all the hassle out of publishing, delivering a higher quality end product with a lot less stress than I could ever achieve on my own."*

    - Keith Corbett, Woodland Wellness and author of *The HEART Manifesto: How to Master the Law of Attraction To Create the Life You Want*

 *"The breadth of Donna's expertise became very apparent when we began working together on my book project. The quality and depth of her work couldn't have been a better match. She helped me find my voice and move into getting the word out, while creating ease every step of the way. Not only that, with her stellar support my book soared to become a #1 Amazon International Bestseller in four categories! Her follow through is bar none, I couldn't have done it without her!"*

    - Rebecca Beardsley, Hair Stylist Mentor and Salon Owner and author of *Self-Care for Hairdressers: How to Prevent Stress and Burnout and Step Into the Professional You Were Meant To Be*

 *"As most authors these days, I decided to publish my own book and it was a steep learning curve but a great journey. After talking with Donna, I instantly liked her confidence and what she could do for me. It had always been a dream - to become a best-seller author, and Donna made it possible. I had to pinch myself when Donna emailed the day after the launch and told me it*

had become an INTERNATIONAL Amazon best-seller. I was living my dream! If you want to be productive and do it right, give it to the right people like Donna, the investment is well worth it and that credibility is something that you will carry for the rest of your life. I was very impressed when my story got into major media sites - now that in itself is worth gold!
- Zaheen Nanji, Co-Owner, Shanti Wellness Centre and author of *The Resilience Reflex: 8 Keys to Transforming Barriers into Success in Life and Business*

 *"Donna really knows how get powerful results. I worked with her as a co-author on the **Biz Smart Quick Guide: 10 Strategies to Online Visibility for More Traffic, Clicks and Profit!** She made the entire process a joy. She provided terrific insight, ideas, and proven methods for making the book a number one bestseller. Having a number one best seller under my belt has already made a huge difference in my business. I'd jump at the chance to work with her again."*
- Shonda Taylor, Business Coach, co-author of Biz Smart Quick Guide: 10 Strategies to Online Visibility for More Traffic, Clicks and Profit

Table of Contents

Are You a Best-Kept Secret?

LOOKING TO GO FROM best-kept secret to business famous? In the age of Google, being known as the go-to person in your industry is essential.

If you....

- Are tired of your competition getting all your customers, even though you know you are much better than they are
- Wish you could break out of the commodity trap
- Want more clients to seek you out...you are certainly not alone!

The biggest reason you may have picked up this book is that you feel like you're in survival mode and are always out looking for new clients or customers. It's either feast or famine kind of situation.

One of the issues you might be facing in this scenario is that you have no perceived credibility or authority in the eyes of your prospects. What do I mean by that? If you are what I term "the obvious choice" or the authority in your industry, prospects trust you and buy from you or hire you without you having to take them through a traditional sales process to move them from prospect to customer.

When you become the obvious choice, prospects start chasing you instead of you chasing them. The lead - prospect - customer conversion process is easier, and the percentage of prospect to customer conversions are much higher. Customers will be eager to refer you to everyone they know.

The secret in making your prospects choose you is easy to do. It's not as difficult as the gurus might tell you. And, when used correctly, it will dramatically position you as the obvious "go to authority."

What's the secret? Become Business Famous. No, I don't mean like a celebrity on the cover of *People* magazine.

Instead, you'll be recognized as a leader and trusted authority in your area of business and your community. How do you accomplish this? By using one of the most powerful marketing tools in the world that has been around for centuries.

What is this tool?

A short book with you as the author that you can use as the ultimate business card and a lead magnet for your business.

The book is in a unique format that is specifically designed to start the sales conversation with your perfect prospects by addressing the most common fears, misconceptions, and obstacles with which you can help them.

Think of it almost like an introductory meeting you'd have with your perfect prospect. Some call it a "strategy session" or a "free consultation."

Your book will be that meeting in a short, easy-to-read format that you can print for a little more than the cost of a brochure and hand out to prospective clients. I call this a lead-generation book. Lead-generation books are all-stars at helping create business and brand domination.

Don't worry if you think you can't write or don't know anything about creating a book. Over the last 20 years, I've helped hundreds of business owners amp up their online visibility and build their brand, and one thing I've realized is that there are a lot of common questions and concerns at the beginning of any new marketing strategy.

I've also seen a lot of people make some costly mistakes that could have easily been avoided if they just had the right information and answers to their questions.

That's why I wrote this short book – to help you navigate your way through the maze and make an informed decision about using your own lead-generation book to get more clients, referrals, and visibility for your local business.

You'll find no fluff, no technical jargon -- only straight information you want to know and NEED to know before deciding to publish a lead-generation book to promote your business.

I'll cover the benefits, pros, and cons, and answer the most pressing questions I get about publishing your own lead-generation book.

Let me be clear. While this book is packed full of valuable information about the most common issues you may be facing, it doesn't have all the answers. That would be impossible, as the truth is there is no single right answer for everyone.

Even though the differences may be small, every situation is unique. So, if you have a question or concern that's not addressed in this book, I'm here to help. You can reach me at 409-450-1950 or shoot me an email at support@bizsmart-media.com.

I'm confident that together we can find a solution.

Let's get started!
Donna Gunter

What Kinds of Business Owners Benefit from a Book?

BECOMING THE AUTHOR OF your own book will help you if you are a business owner, consultant, speaker, coach, or professional service provider in fields like:

Legal
- Bankruptcy
- Business Formation
- Divorce Lawyers
- Estate Planning
- Personal Injury

Real Estate
- Home Appraisers
- Home Inspectors
- Home Stagers
- Foreclosure/Short Sale
- Mortgage Brokers
- Real Estate Investors
- Realtors

Health/Beauty
- Alternative medicine practitioners
- Chiropractors
- Cosmetic Surgery
- Day spas
- Dental
- Dermatologists
- Dieticians
- Gyms
- Hair replacement
- Hair salons
- Massage Therapists
- Personal Trainers
- Weight loss specialists

Insurance
- Annuities
- Car
- Commercial
- Home
- Independent Agents
- Life

Home Services
- Air Conditioning/Heating
- Bathroom Remodeling
- Decks & Porches
- Electrician
- Fencing
- Flooring
- General Contractors
- Handyman
- Heating and Cooling
- Home Theater Services
- HVAC
- Interior Designers
- Kitchen Remodeling
- Landscaping
- Painters
- Plumbers
- Pools & Spas

- Roofing
- Security Systems
- Siding

Professional Services
- Accountants/CPAs
- Consultants
- Financial Planners
- HR Specialists

Events
- Catering
- Florists
- Disc Jockeys
- Limousine Service
- Personal Chefs
- Photography/Videography
- Weddings
- Wedding Planners

Miscellaneous
- Childcare
- Martial Arts School
- Pet Groomers
- Professional Organizers
- Tattoo shops

- Veterinarians
- Anyone in a competitive consulting or professional services field

And, it's useful for anyone who is currently using business cards, brochures, flyers, and advertising on local television and radio stations as the ways of promoting your business.

I'm a <Your Occupation>. Why Should I Publish a Book?

FIRST AND FOREMOST, YOU want to build credibility and authority in your local area. Let's talk about what most business owners do in their businesses to build authority and build credibility:

- Pay for advertising on local television and radio stations or newspapers
- Take out ads on billboards, sides of buses, or bus benches
- Create expensive cards, brochures, and flyers and drop them everywhere
- Hire expensive SEO firms to boost your website's search engine rankings

- Ask for testimonials and reviews from customers
- Create an educational video series
- Get interviewed on TV, radio, and podcasts
- Hold a series of Lunch and Learns
- Go to many networking events

The big challenge with all those strategies is they take a long time to create and implement. For many of them, you cannot determine your ROI (Return on Investment). You can build your authority, credibility, and visibility using these strategies and get where you want to be, but it's going to take you some time to get some traction. Most of us don't want to spend three months, six months, nine months, or a year trying to get that kind of traction. We need to really explode our businesses.

That's why the easiest and best way to build massive authority, instant credibility, and create a fantastic lead magnet for your business is your own world-class lead book with your name on it as the author. Best of all, it can be created without having to spend massive amounts of time and money, even if you hate to write.

Will This Book Be More Effective Than the Brochures, Flyers, or Swag I Give Away?

THERE IS STILL A significant amount of awe that comes with being the author of a published book. Unlike business cards and brochures, when you hand out books, recipients won't throw them away.

Think back to conferences and networking events you have attended. How many of the business cards, brochures, glossy folders, or swag (pens, water bottles, keychains, mouse pads, and the like that are imprinted with your business name) have you collected and thrown out? If you're like me, I toss most of it in the trash after I return from an event. It doesn't really serve me, and the material adds too much clutter to my life.

However, when you hand out a book, conversations change in an instant. Recipients will keep your book on their bookshelves or desks and look at them repeatedly, or perhaps pass them along to friends and family who might be seeking a solution to the problem solved in your book. They may get a little star-struck and ask you to autograph the book. Little else establishes trust and credibility more readily than being a published author of your own book.

With a published book, you will have created:

1. **Ultimate Business Card**. Books are a great marketing tool that allows you to reach out to a broader audience and provide them with a solution to one of their significant problems. When you publish a book about your expertise, you can give or sell copies to people during public speaking opportunities or even distribute them online. When you give your book to someone, they instantly become pre-sold on you before you open your mouth, and you then become the welcomed guest rather than a pest who is trying to sell yourself or your services.

2. Automatic Pre-Qualified Lead Generation. Give a copy of your book to all your current clients and prospects to begin the lead generation process. When selling or giving your book away, be sure and collect your prospect's information and add that to your database (with permission, of course) so that you can follow up with that prospect in the future.

If you are selling your book via a third-party source, like Amazon, add a page at the beginning of your book that offers a valuable follow-up gift (video, audio, checklist, webinar) that goes into more detail about one of the points in your book. Ask readers for their names and email addresses in exchange for your offer.

3. Media Darling. Your book serves as a source of quality information for getting quoted in magazines, newspapers, and online blogs. Most radio and television stations and podcasts love having authors as guests on the shows they host. Therefore, a book can provide you with some fantastic opportunities for free media exposure, which no other marketing channel can offer.

4. Credibility. Publishing a book provides you with instant expert status. Other people will now view you as an authority on your topic, as there is still a certain aura of respect, awe, and credibility that follows anyone who is a published author. A book will give credence to your expert status, as you knew enough about a topic to publish a book on it.

5. **Increased Referrals**. Customers trust authors who have written a book on their subject of expertise. Writing a book provides you and your business with increased public exposure and credibility. If you are using your book as your business card, give an additional copy or two and ask the recipient to distribute them to others that might need your expertise. This helps to increase the number of referrals for your business.

6. **You, the Obvious Choice**. From increasing your brand's visibility to increasing your referrals and improving your customer loyalty, writing a book provides you with an edge over your competition, most of whom (if not all) have not written their own book. The increased credibility also sets you apart from your competition, which will help to make you the obvious choice when a prospect is seeking a solution to the problem that you solve.

7. **Cost-Effective Marketing Tool.** If you are currently doing any print, radio, television or

pay-per-click (PPC) advertising, offer a copy of your book as the advertisement's call to action, rather than focusing on selling your products or services in the ad. Your book acts as your long sales letter, business card, display ad, and credibility builder, all rolled up into one, and can dramatically increase both the quantity and quality of leads you collect for your business.

8. **Lead as an Educator and Advocate**. Being an educator and an advocate for your clients is much easier than marketing yourself as a product or service. As an entrepreneur, you possess a specific set of skills and knowledge that are unique to you, your business, and the problem that you solve. Publishing a one-problem, one-solution book allows you to offer quality information to prospects to help them solve a specific problem and expertly position yourself to your clients.

9. **Increased Customer Retention**. By writing a book, you provide your customers with a tangible reminder of who you are. If you are in a business in which someone might forget your name because they don't use your service that often (like a real estate agent, for example), your

book will remind your customer to seek you out to do business with you again.

10. **Increased Revenue**. Writing a book helps to improve your marketing opportunities and generate more leads, which increases your revenue. It can also open new additional income streams such as consulting, speaking, and product creation opportunities. The new expert status gained from publishing a book also allows you to charge more fees without the risk of losing customers; clients will pay more for an established expert.

Whatever your goal in writing your book, the bottom line is that a book offers quality content that customers crave. It can also increase your marketing opportunities and generate more revenue for your business, thus creating the option for exponential growth. Best of all, you can integrate your book into most of your current marketing activities and make them more effective.

CHAPTER 4

How Will This Book Help Me Grow My Business?

THERE IS A HUGE book publishing myth that stops a lot of people in their tracks or sends them down the rabbit hole searching for something that's not realistic at all. That myth is that you are going to make thousands or millions of dollars from selling your book. Let me tell you right now -- that is dead wrong. That is not the purpose of your book.

Instead, the book publishing reality is that you should give away as many copies of your book as you possibly can, and don't worry about selling the book.

Think of it this way. Would you rather get commissions as a real estate agent from sales of

$300,000 properties, or would you instead try and sell the equivalent number of books priced at $19.99 to equal those commissions? If used properly, your book can create that kind of business for you by making sure it gets into the hands of the right prospects.

The new model of book publishing is all about positioning yourself as the authority in your local area and making money on the back end as a result of putting your books into as many hands as possible. We are not looking for you to become a celebrity throughout the United States. We're looking for you to become a local celebrity recognized by the people you interact with daily - your neighbors, your family, your friends, and your acquaintances at church and in civic and professional organizations.

Your book makes you an educator and advocate for your clients. One of the best ways to market your business is as an educator and advocate. I discovered this accidentally years ago by liberally sharing "how-to" business information on various online article banks and sites. When you are the educator and advocate, you begin to build loyalty. The come to you for information and guidance, and you become a valuable resource. When they are ready to solve the problem for which you provide the solution, guess who they will think of first?

For example, if you wanted to position yourself as the leader in landscaping and lawn care in your local area, you could blog about what types of native plants should be introduced at what time of year. Or, perhaps you offer tips on how to naturally repel harmful bugs from the shrubbery. This information not only helps customers, but it also confirms your status as an expert in your field - and potentially lead to more sales. When you put this information info a book, you become unstoppable!

CHAPTER 5

How Will This Book Help Me Generate Pre-Qualified Leads?

SAVVY ENTREPRENEURS ARE USING their books as the foundation of the businesses. They are publishing a book to make themselves an ACE (Authority, Credibility, Expert). They are using this book to set themselves up as the obvious choice for their target market and distinguish themselves from their competitors.

For example, if you wanted to find a dentist who does teeth whitening, wouldn't you pay more attention to the dentist who had written a book on the subject, especially if he offered to send the book to you at no charge? The key to monetizing your book is to ensure that it gets into as many hands of your target prospect as possible.

For most business owners, this means giving the book away as a promotional offer. For example, rather than creating a commercial advertising his teeth whitening services on a local TV station's channel, a local dentist will focus the content of the television ad on his book about teeth whitening and tell viewers where they can get their free copy.

He will take out a similar advertisement in a local magazine, where the ad focuses on the reader requesting a copy of his book on teeth whitening. Similarly, he'll make the same offer of a free book as the lead magnet on his website.

What is happening when the prospect gets the book? Unlike a business card or a brochure, the prospect is reading, or at least skimming the book when he receives it, and the prospect tends to keep the book on his desk or in his bookshelf and not throw it in the trash, which is the fate of so many kinds of marketing materials.

As the prospect reads the book, he is unconsciously absorbing the dentist's expertise, as the dentist has created a short read (55-75 pages) on the topic of teeth whitening. The book is short enough to be easily read in one sitting, like when waiting to pick up kids from school, on the train commuting to work, or at a layover at the airport.

Because the prospect hangs onto the book, s/he is reminded about the service the dentist offers every time he sees the book around his home or office. When the prospect is ready to move forward on getting his teeth whitened, more than likely s/he will contact the office of the dentist from whom he received the book. The book generated a qualified lead for the dentist.

If the dentist has an automated system of follow-up messages or mailings to those prospects requesting the book, it's almost a certainty that the prospect will choose the dentist who wrote the book as the dentist to do the teeth whitening.

Teeth whitening costs an average of $600. How many books sold at $19.95 would the dentist have had to sell to make that same money? The answer is 19. Moreover, once the prospect becomes a patient and if the new patient is happy with the dentist and the teeth whitening process, the likelihood that this patient will return to the dentist for other types of services is much higher.

Remember, it costs much less to retain a current patient than to continually prospect for new patients. With the lifetime customer value of a dental patient estimated to be $10,000, can you see how using his book as a lead generator is making the dentist much more revenue than trying to sell individual books?

CHAPTER 6

If a Book is Effective, Why Aren't All Business Owners Doing It?

THERE ARE SEVERAL ROADBLOCKS preventing business people from publishing their own book. Many simply just don't know what to do and where to begin, or they are overwhelmed with trying to manage too many details.

They might think it takes too long, it costs too much, or believe there's no way they can do this because they hate to write, don't write well, or are dyslexic. Or, they might simply fear putting themselves out there because they have never done anything like this before. They are not quite sure what reaction they are going to get if they declare themselves to be an authority on some topic. Or, they might be afraid that nobody will read the book once it's published. Many think that to be published, they would have to get an agent and a publisher and write the book themselves.

All of these are common roadblocks and misconceptions about publishing a book. Let's get over those hurdles right now.

CHAPTER 7

What If I'm Not Qualified to Write a 250-Page Book?

THE OLD PUBLISHING MODEL says that you must have this great tome of a book, 250 pages written about all aspects of a problem, essentially the "everything guide" to a topic. With the new publishing model, 50 - 75 pages are perfect for a one-problem, one-solution lead-generation book for your target market.

A commonly held mistaken belief is that authors can only write helpful and relevant books with academic or professional "credentials" or "qualifications." This may have been true at one time, but today the premium is on experience and an ability to provide useful information to a market that wants the information.

Surprisingly enough, a 45-60-minute conversation about a topic is the perfect amount of content that is needed for such a book. And, don't think of this process as writing a book. Instead, you're having a conversation with an ideal prospect who already needs to solve a particular problem and is just trying to decide who to hire to solve that problem.

Let's look realistically at these 250-page books versus the 70-page books. A successful short book is something that someone can read on a commute to a job, whether they're taking the bus, the train, the subway, or can be read on an airplane ride or while waiting to pick up the kids from school or during a child's sports practice.

Think back now -- how many business books have you started? When I read business books, I usually go to the chapter that seems to apply most to whatever problem I'm experiencing and then never read the rest.

When you have a much shorter book, the likelihood of people finishing that book is much, much more significant than having that "everything guide to plastic surgery" that no one will ever complete.

CHAPTER 8

Don't I Need to Find a Publisher Who Will Publish My Book?

IN THE OLD MODEL of publishing, that was the way it was done. You needed an agent to find a publisher, and then it would take a minimum of a year, usually closer to two years, before your book would be printed. The industry then moved to vanity publishing where you would hire a publisher who would force you to buy 5,000 copies of your book as a part of your book publishing contract. For many authors, those books would sit collecting dust in their garages.

The new publishing model gives you print-on-demand (POD) self-publishing, which saves you much money and time. You don't have closets or garages full of books. Instead, you can simply print the book when you need it. That's precisely the model that Amazon follows, which is my print-on-demand partner via their POD service, Kindle Direct Publishing (KDP).

For the books published via KDP, Amazon doesn't keep all those titles available on their website sitting in some humongous warehouse someplace. They print a book when they have an order for the book.

In the old publishing model, self-promotion within your book is highly discouraged. The traditional publisher doesn't let you mention your programs, your services, or your products in your book. They give you a bio page at the back of the book as the only place where you can tell readers about yourself.

In the new publishing model, you can do pretty much whatever you want to do inside your book, as you control the content. You can list links to your website and social media profiles. You can make a special offer just for readers at the beginning of your book. You can encourage readers to buy your products and services or hire you to speak at an event.

All these promotional opportunities are the secret sauce that makes your book an effective lead magnet. With the POD publishing model, you don't have any of those traditional publisher self-promotion restrictions with which to deal.

How Difficult is It to Publish My Own Book?

SELF-PUBLISHING INVOLVES AN extensive list of tasks. The answer to that question depends on how much of the work you want to do yourself. You can choose to do it all yourself, outsource many of the tasks, or hire a POD publishing expert who will do most of the work for you.

Here's a list of what's involved:

Writing Process
- Choose the topic of your book
- Create an outline of the chapters of the book

- Take at least 30 minutes per day to write the book
- Complete the manuscript

Pre-Publication Process
- Edit or obtain editing for your manuscript
- Proofread or get proofreading for your manuscript
- Obtain any artwork or illustrations you wish to include
- Obtain ISBN and Library of Congress "Cataloging in Publication" numbers

Publication Process
- Format manuscript (design interior layout, including appropriate margins, headers/footers, typeface, interior art/graphics, etc.)
- Provide "front matter" (table of contents, copyright page) and back matter (content on the back of the book)
- Provide or obtain cover art; design front and back covers (including "cover blurbs" or reviews) and spine.

- Obtain printing quotes (including trim size, number of pages, binding, paper quality, etc.) for print books
- Determine the format in which manuscript must be delivered to the printer
- Arrange/pay for printing and delivery of finished books.

Post-Publication Process
- Continue with an ongoing marketing campaign.
- Send books to reviewers.
- Receive and store printed books. (Clear out your garage!)
- Handle order fulfillment: Receive orders, process payments, invoice customers for amounts due, package and ship, or transmit books.

However, you don't have to do this alone. When you hire a certified book publishing coach who specializes in publishing print-on-demand books for business owners, the amount of the time you must invest in the book production process is reduced from hundreds of hours to about three hours total.

CHAPTER 10

How Much Time Will This Take?

OUR PROCESS IS DESIGNED to let you focus on running your business, so ideally, you won't spend more than about three hours dealing with details of the book.

Here's an approximate breakdown of your time:

- 45 minutes: Initial meeting to determine the goal, audience, focus, and topic of the book
- 45 minutes: participating in the interview for your book

- 30 minutes: providing information about and feedback on the cover of the book
- 60 minutes: reviewing the final copy of the book
- **Total time investment: about 3 hours**

Three hours for the opportunity to potentially double or triple your revenue, generate more pre-qualified leads, increase your referrals – isn't that a high ROI (Return on Investment) for your time?

Which Is Better, Print Books or Ebooks?

THE ANSWER TO THIS question is, "it depends." Each format has its own advantages and disadvantages. The primary benefit of print publication is that print books have a much wider audience than electronic books, regardless of the topic or genre. Most of the book-buying public (and your potential market) still prefer physical books and buys them through non-electronic channels. And, for promotional purposes as a local business owner, print books work more effectively.

The primary advantage of electronic books is the low cost (or, indeed, near absence of cost) to produce them. Even if you choose to pay for professional cover design and formatting (a good idea), your price per book will be extremely low. An e-book may exist as nothing more than a computer file that can be e-mailed to the customer or downloaded from a website. Even if you choose to distribute the book on disk or CD-ROM, your production costs are far less than for a print book (as are your shipping costs).

If you are choosing to write a book, having your book available as both a print and ebook will permit you to maximize your marketing opportunities.

CHAPTER 12

How Long Will It Take to See a Printed Copy My Book?

WE STRIVE TO WORK hard and get your book published as quickly as possible. Provided that you respond in a timely fashion to our requests for the interview, cover review, content review, and electronic proof review, you can have your book in hand in as few as 60 days.

However, to account for unforeseen difficulties, plan for the longest time it will take (90 days) and know that we will strive to get your book in hand in 60 days if possible.

After reviewing the electronic (PDF) proof, we will send you a print proof copy so that you can hold a physical copy of the book in your hands. We'll ask you to review that proof to ensure everything is laid out in the way you desire. Depending on the number of changes required, we may order a second print proof to let see and hold the updated version.

The proof versions are printed with a "Not For Resale" banner across the cover. This will not be present in the final version of your book.

Once the proofing process is completed, we'll send you a copy of the final print version of your book.

CHAPTER 13

How Do I Write My Book?

THERE ARE SEVERAL WAYS you can do this, and some are easier than others:

- Sit down for a set time each day and write your book. This is the hard way.
- Transcribe past media interviews as the basis for your book. You can then organize the content into a short, easily readable book.
- Repurpose content from your blog or other content from your website or from your brochures into a short book.

Or, you can do this the easy way, which requires no writing at all on your part. You can sit for a 45-60-minute interview for a book that is specifically designed to start sales conversations. Don't think of this as another "book." It's more of a direct marketing tool. Think of it like a printed version of a strategy session or free consultation that is cheap to print and hand out (or even mail) to leads. We refer to this type of book as a lead-generation book because its purpose is to generate pre-qualified leads.

In fact, this book you are reading is an example of a lead-generation book.

CHAPTER 14

What About Copyrights and Editing?

WITH OUR PUBLISHING PROCESS, the author retains the copyright to the book and all the intellectual property within. The contracts with most traditional publishers, unless you get an exclusion, force you to limit the amount of material you can use in your book for other purposes, like course creation or training or speaking gigs.

However, we hold no such exclusionary rights in our contract. As the intellectual property owner and the copyright owner, you can do whatever you like with your intellectual property above and beyond using the content in your book.

We will meet with you to get ideas on your cover design as well as on the topic of your book. You will also get the opportunity to proof the final manuscript of the book in both electronic and print formats before it goes to press.

You don't have to hire a professional editor for us to publish your book. Our editors provide free developmental editing, copyediting, line editing, and proofreading services to our authors.

Do I Get Input on the Cover?

YOUR BOOK COVER AND manuscript interior layout will be designed by our team. but you have full creative control. You will get a beautiful cover design because having a great book cover is key to establishing your book as credible and professional.

Before we start the design process, you'll be asked a series of questions for us to get a feel for your business and your brand. We organize this information and use it to create an initial cover design, on which you will review and give feedback. We'll tweak it until you are happy.

If you have no idea what kind of cover you would like, we will steer you in the direction of recent covers from best-selling books in your genre to help you get a feel for what you want and dislike.

If you're willing, the best cover for your book might be the one that features an image of you!

How Much Will I Pay for Copies of My Book?

WE WON'T CHARGE YOU anything for copies. You get to buy copies at the print cost. These are called author copies. For print on demand paperbacks, Kindle Direct Publishing not only prints books for approximately $2.50 a copy (not including shipping) when they're ordered through Amazon, but they'll sell the author these books at the same cost.

At any time after the book is published, you can order copies in any quantity you'd like at this discounted price, direct from the printer. We don't make money on copies.

If you need to purchase very large quantities of a book (100+) for an event or conference, we'll set up an account for your book at Lulu. Lulu generally offers more competitive pricing when you need to buy a large number of books at one time.

CHAPTER 17

What Royalties Will I Earn?

WE DO NOT PAY any royalties. Since your book will be for sale in the Amazon store, you will receive 100% of the royalties of any books purchased for the retail price directly from Kindle Direct Publishing. You will not be paid any royalties on the author copies you buy at wholesale pricing.

.

How Do I Distribute My Book?

REMEMBER THAT MONETIZATION OF your book is not going to come from book sales. While you may make a few sales of the book, there are more powerful ways to monetize your book. The goal of distributing your book is to make yourself a client magnet - become irresistible to your prospects.

Here are the best ways to produce revenue and grow your business from your book:

Mail your book to your current and prospective clients free of charge. Include a personal note, autograph the book, and choose an eye-catching envelope as the mailer. With the amount of email that we all get these days, snail mail is under-utilized. So, use old school direct mail to draw attention to yourself. When you send your clients and your prospects a book, you become top-of-mind to them. Unlike a business card, business flyer, or business brochure that are quickly thrown out, most people will hang onto a book or pass it along to someone who needs it.

Send your book to local groups and clubs and request to speak at their upcoming meetings. This action instantly puts you at the top of the speaker list for associations and groups because you've got a book and are a published author.

Offer your book as a free lead magnet in your advertising or on your website. Whether you advertise on local media sites or local television or radio stations, make the call to action in your advertisement the opportunity to receive your book. You can offer to send an electronic or print version of the book, or both. By using your book as a lead magnet, you are getting your book into the hands of prospects so they can read about you, your expertise, and your solution to a particular problem they have.

Send the book out to your local media to position yourself as a subject matter expert. Letting your local newspaper, magazine, and television/radio broadcasters and reporters know that you have published a book will get their attention, especially if you add a media release as a part of the mailing you do to the local media. When they need an expert like you in the course of writing a story, you will be top-of-mind as a person to contact for a quote or an appearance on a local show. It makes you worthy to the media and gives them a reason to interview.

Hand out your book at networking meetings. When you give out a copy of your book, that's going to stick much more with people than a business card or brochure. It will help you gain a considerable edge over your competition.

Ultimately, the goal is to get your book into as many hands as possible, whether that's a physical copy or an electronic copy of your book. That's why I want to reiterate that you're not going to make money from the sales of your book. You're going to make money after people have read the book and will then come back and hire you for your services and products.

Where Will My Book Be Sold?

YOUR BOOK WILL BE available for retail sale in both print and electronic formats from Amazon.com. In the publication process, we request expanded distribution from Kindle Direct Publishing to make your book available on other platforms. Please note that it may take 4-6 months for your book to be listed in these other platforms due to the way Amazon's Expanded Distribution process works.

However, please remember that you will get the most ROI out of your book by giving it out to current customers, vendors and referral partners, as well as using it as a lead generator in any advertising efforts. While it will be listed for sale online, book sales should not be your ultimate goal in publishing a book for your business.

If you decide to give away the electronic version of your book on your website or as a part of your advertising efforts, we can make your book available in a variety of downloadable formats appropriate to be viewed on a computer, smartphone, or tablet.

CHAPTER 20

Can You Get My Books into a Bookstore?

MOST RETAIL BOOKSTORES WILL not carry a self-published book unless you have sold at least 25,000 copies. We do not automatically put your book in bookstores. However, Amazon's Expanded Distribution program will make it available for bookstores to order through other platforms.

We don't deny that going into a bookstore and seeing your book on the shelf is nice, but having a book in a bookstore does almost nothing in terms of sales or awareness. It is only a status object.

If you want your book carried in local bookstores, you should directly approach the bookstore owner or manager and see if you can work out a deal for them to stock the book. They may ask you to let them carry the book on consignment rather than buying the books outright.

However, this conversation may lead to you holding a book signing at their store. That would be a great event to which you invite friends, family, colleagues, associates, vendors, customers, and prospects!

How Do I Choose a Topic for My Book?

REMEMBER, THINK OF YOUR book as having a conversation with an ideal prospect who already needs to solve a particular problem and is just trying to decide who to hire to solve that problem. You will be speaking to your perfect prospects by addressing the most common fears, misconceptions, and obstacles with which you can help them.

In a nutshell, your book needs to answer the following questions that your ideal prospect has about your program or service:

- Does the person (you) understand my problem?
- Is the person qualified to solve my problem?
- Is my problem unique - will this solution work for me?
- What is the risk to find out more?

Below is a series of questions for you to consider as a quick action plan to getting your own published book underway:

1. Who is your perfect prospect for the book?
2. What three services or products are the most profitable for your business or are the ones that make you happiest to deliver?
3. Pick your favorite/most profitable service or product, or one that best solves what your perfect prospect wants to achieve.
4. What are the 3-5 ways you solve a customer/client's problem with that offering?
5. Pick one of the solutions you provide that offers information about how your perfect prospect solves that problem.

6. What are the top 10 frequently asked questions that you commonly get about that service or product?
7. What is your call to action/offer for anyone reading your book? This should be something not readily available anywhere else in your marketing materials. Make your readers feel valued and unique.

If you'd like to get a worksheet to help you with this action plan, request our reader bonuses at https://MakeThemChooseYou.com/bonus.

Here are some sample industries with effective lead-generation book topics:

- Caterer: Using Catering for a School Graduation
- Dentist: Teeth Whitening for Brides
- Property Manager: Property Management for Rental Property Owners
- Real estate agent: Preparing Your Home for Sale
- HVAC: HVAC Maintenance for Homeowners
- Divorce attorney: Using Mediation to Resolve Your Divorce

- Chiropractor: Importance of Chiropractic Care After an Auto Accident
- Plastic surgeon: Post-Mastectomy Breast Reconstruction
- Plumber: Installing Tankless Water Heaters
- Mortgage Loan officer: Qualifying for Home Loans for Veterans
- Insurance agent- Choosing the Right Homeowner's Insurance

Based on your initial action plan, we begin by setting a meeting with you to discuss your book and go over our publishing process and pricing for your book in a Book Profits session. If you choose to proceed after the meeting, we send a publishing contract. Once the contract is signed, we move forward with the project.

If you're ready, you can set up a complimentary, no-obligation Book Profits session here: https://bizsmartpublishing.com/apply/

What Services Do You Provide?

ALL OUR BOOK PUBLISHING services are provided as a part of our book publishing package fee for our authors.

These services include:

- Help with book title ideas and selection
- Interview to create book content
- Editing the interview into a short, lead-generation book
- Proofreading and copyediting the manuscript
- Cover design
- Formatting and publishing for eBooks

- Interior book design and layout for print books
- Publication of ebook and print book through Kindle Direct Publishing
- An Amazon Best-Selling Book campaign to launch your book's release
- Book monetization training

Other optional services that you can purchase include:

- Audiobook narration, editing, mastering, and publishing
- Book website design and landing page design
- Email marketing systems
- Outreach to U.S. national media outlets via regular media releases
- Regular interviews with podcast and radio show influencers
- Print and online media kits
- Ongoing marketing advice, mentorship, and guidance

We also offer some less expensive book publishing options, including our Done-For-You licensed books and our Multi-Author books. For more details, visit https://bizsmartpublishing.com/done-for-you-books/.

Please refer to our publishing site, https://www.BizSmartPublishing.com and our primary website, https://www.BizSmartMedia.com, for more details on our publishing, promotion, and authority media branding services.

CHAPTER 23

What Will Happen in My Business When I Become Published?

HERE'S WHAT YOU CAN look forward to after publishing your own book:

You'll no longer be AN expert. Instead, you'll be **THE** expert in your local market. You'll get invited on local television and radio shows. It's much easier for a producer to justify the appearance of a published author on their morning talk show than "some guy who says he knows a lot about something."

Your opinion will count for more, and you'll be taken more seriously. After all, they can reference your book after every quote. You'll get more clients. Whatever your business, if you're "published," then prospective clients will seek you out more avidly and engage more readily.

You'll get more invitations to speak. If you want to be up on stage, then there's nothing that says "this person is trustworthy" more than a book published with your name on it. After all, you must know what you're talking about to have a book, right?

You can charge more for whatever it is that you do. Get published, triple your rates, and finally charge what you're worth. Prospects will be more inclined to fork out a little more for a true specialist, whether it's a dentist or accountant or an architect.

You'll be quoted. People who don't like what you've said will quote you, and people who love what you've said will quote you.

Your search engine optimization (SEO) rankings will increase. The more people are talking about you in your local community, the more searches will be conducted for you and your book, and potentially the more backlinks you'll get from high-traffic sites.

You'll have a much better business card than anyone else. While the other business owners are handing out scads of cards which are rapidly discarded and forgotten, you'll be able to hand out copies of your book. And almost no one throws away a good book!

Your signature speech is ready-made. Repurpose what's in your book to speak from the stage at local civic and professional association meetings. Repurpose it again for a workshop for your clients/customers. If appropriate, you can also repurpose it for an online self-study program.

Automatic credibility. Who's going to argue with the person who literally wrote the book on it?

Now, aren't you ready to get started?

CHAPTER 24

Getting Started Checklist

☐ Review all questions answered in this book.

☐ Write down any questions that are not answered.

☐ Determine your goal for publishing a book.

☐ Determine your budget for the book publishing and printing process. Include fees for hiring a book publisher, wholesale book purchases, and marketing.

☐ Complete your Book Action Plan (found in Chapter 21) or download it from https://MakeThemChooseYou.com/bonus.

☐ Set up a complimentary, no-obligation Book Profits session here: https://bizsmartpublishing.com/apply

BONUSES FOR READERS

As a gift for my readers, I have several bonuses you can download at:

https://MakeThemChooseYou.com/bonus

ABOUT THE AUTHOR

Donna Gunter, Amazon #1 best-selling author of *Brand Yourself as the Trusted Local Celebrity* and *Biz Smart Quick Guide: 10 Strategies to Online Visibility for More Traffic, Clicks and Profit!*, helps entrepreneurs, consultants, speakers, coaches and professionals stop the client chase by leveraging their knowledge to gain authority status in their industry, then dramatically amplify their message and shows them how to convert the new audience into high-paying customers.

Using her proven Become Business Famous signature seven-step system, she works together with her clients to build powerful personal brands and grow their businesses through speaking, publishing, and publicity.

WEBSITE: https://www.BizSmartMedia.com
FACEBOOK: https://www.facebook.com/BizSmartMedia
TWITTER: https://twitter.com/donnagunter
LINKEDIN: https://www.linkedin.com/in/donnagunter

OTHER BOOKS BY DONNA GUNTER

https://www.bizsmartmedia.com/localceleb

https://www.bizsmartmedia.com/littlebook

https://www.bizsmartmedia.com/bizsmartquick